# CONTENTS

Football words are explained in the glossary on page 30.

# I AM A FOOTBALL FREAK

Joe Flynn Fact File:
**Age:** Fourteen
**Position:** Striker
**My Team:** Dynamos
**Favourite Team:** Manchester United (and England)
**Favourite Player:** David Beckham

This is me!

I'm Joe Flynn and football is my life. I play or watch football whenever it's possible. The coming season is going to be more exciting than ever, and with so much going on I thought I'd better write it all down!

My favourite player has got to be David Beckham. He's a great player and he always looks so cool too! I don't suppose he ever kept a diary but if he did I bet it would be worth a lot of money now. There's a thought!

DAVID BECKHAM

Nickname: Becks

Born: 2 May 1975

Clubs: Preston North End, Manchester United, Real Madrid

United debut: 7 December 1994, European Cup v Galatasaray

England debut: 1 September 1996, World Cup qualifier v Moldova

When I can't get out and play I seek inspiration in magazines.

**THIS SEASON I MUST:**
- Buy new boots and kit.
- Clean my boots.
- Score at least 20 goals.
- Work on the weaknesses in my game.
- Help the Dynamos finish higher than fourth.

Waiting for training – and I still can't stop practising!

5

## JULY

|   |    |    |    |
|---|----|----|----|
|   | 7  | 14 | 21 | 28 |
| 1 | 8  | 15 | 22 | 29 |
| 2 | 9  | 16 | 23 | 30 |
| 3 | 10 | 17 | 24 | 31 |
| 4 | 11 | 18 | 25 |
| 5 | 12 | 19 | 26 |
| 6 | 13 | 20 | 27 |

Me chesting the ball.

## SATURDAY 26 JULY
## KICKABOUTS

We've just finished school for the summer – thank goodness! In the summer I can stay out and play football until it gets dark, and now school has finished I can play in the day too. Yes!

A bunch of us got together last night and played a really good game of Headers and Volleys. It's a bit chaotic, but I really want my headers to get better this season, so I was concentrating on doing as many of those as possible.

### HEADERS AND VOLLEYS

We'll usually play Headers and Volleys if there aren't many of us. We play first to score five and then swap goalkeepers. The outfield players can only score from a header or a volley, and only if the ball reaches them without bouncing. If the goalkeeper catches the ball without it bouncing he gets a goal.

6

Steven about to score in a five-a-side game, which is what we usually play if there are enough people. Coach says it's not all about scoring goals but I'm glad I'm not a defender!

Last winter we played on the all-weather pitch when the park got too muddy.

If there aren't many of us we play Rush Goalie, when the nearest defender to the goal can use his hands and be goalie. You can play Stick Goalie too, when the same person has to stay in goal until someone else takes over.

## JULY

```
      7   14   21  (28)
 1    8   15   22   29
 2    9   16   23   30
 3   10   17   24   31
 4   11   18   25
 5   12   19   26
 6   13   20   27
```

## MONDAY 28 JULY
## NEW KIT

I went into town to get some new kit today. My other kit was getting tatty, and a bit small. There's a shop on the High Street that specialises in football stuff. I told them what I wanted and how much I wanted to spend and they helped me find what I needed.

In the end I got new boots, clothes and shinpads, so now I'm all set. Can't wait until Dynamos training starts again. We've been given new team kit too. That should help us! We finished fourth in the league last time around but I reckon we can do better next season.

LIGHT, COMFORTABLE AND DURABLE BOOTS — JUST WHAT I NEED! THESE ONES LOOK PRETTY COOL, TOO...

THE BOOTS HAVE SCREW-IN STUDS FOR BETTER GRIP. I'LL WEAR MY TRAINERS IF THE GROUND IS DRY AND HARD, BUT THAT WON'T HAPPEN MUCH IN A BRITISH SUMMER!

8

I WANTED A PAIR OF
SHINPADS WITH ANKLE
PROTECTORS, BECAUSE AS A
STRIKER I'M ALWAYS GETTING
KICKED IN THE ANKLES BY
DEFENDERS. THEY'RE A BIT
HEAVY, BUT IT BEATS
GETTING BRUISED LEGS.

OUR NEW TEAM
KIT. I'M WELL
PLEASED WITH IT.
I PREFER
LONG-SLEEVED
SHIRTS.

I'm sure I'll play
better in this!

## AUGUST

| | | | |
|---|---|---|---|
| 4 | 11 | 18 | 25 |
| 5 | 12 | 19 | 26 |
| 6 | 13 | 20 | 27 |
| 7 | 14 | 21 | 28 |
| 1 | 8 | 15 | 22 | 29 |
| 2 | 9 | 16 | 23 | 30 |
| 3 | 10 | 17 | 24 | 31 |

**THIGH STRETCH**
PULL ONE FOOT UP YOUR
BACK, KNEE BENT.
PUSH HIPS GENTLY
FORWARD AND HOLD.
TO BALANCE, LEAN
AGAINST TEAM—MATE.

# SATURDAY 9 AUGUST
# FIRST TRAINING
# SESSION

At last, our first proper training
session! We warmed up by
jogging, then we did some
stretching and finally some
sprinting. I can't believe it was
half-an-hour before we kicked a
ball! Feeling a bit tired.

Must remember to stretch
before and after training and
matches. The last thing I want
to do is get injured, which is
what will happen if I go out and
play with 'cold muscles'. I found
these warm-up stretches in
a book:

**HAMSTRING
STRETCH**
POSITION LEGS AN
ARM'S LENGTH APART.
LEGS STRAIGHT,
TOUCH THE GROUND.
MOVE HANDS
FROM ONE FOOT
TO ANOTHER.

**CALF STRETCH**
FEET APART, FACING FORWARD,
ONE AHEAD OF THE OTHER.
LEAN FORWARD, FRONT LEG BENT, BACK LEG STRAIGHT.
THIS WORKS BETTER IF YOU LEAN AGAINST A TEAM—MATE.

Colin, our coach, said press-ups and sit-ups will help improve my upper body strength. I'm going to do some every night.

Sprinting along the pitch.

Practising moving the ball between four of us while running. It's harder than it looks.

## AUGUST

| | | | |
|---|---|---|---|
| | 4 | 11 | 18 | 25 |
| | 5 | 12 | 19 | 26 |
| | 6 | 13 | 20 | 27 |
| | 7 | 14 | 21 | 28 |
| 1 | 8 | 15 | 22 | 29 |
| 2 | 9 | 16 | 23 | 30 |
| 3 | 10 | 17 | 24 | 31 |

# SATURDAY 23 AUGUST
# TEAM TACTICS

When we play in the park we don't really pay much attention to tactics, so today's training was a real eye-opener. Now I realise different teams play with different formations. A team looking to attack will put more players forward than a team that is on the defensive.

I think we play a sort of 4–3–3 but really we all mostly just end up chasing the ball!

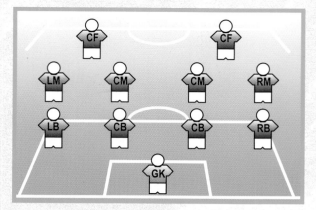

## 4–4–2
MOST POPULAR FORMATION: 4 DEFENDERS, 4 MIDFIELDERS, 2 STRIKERS. THE 2 WIDE MIDFIELDERS PUSH FORWARD WHEN POSSIBLE. ONE STRIKER LINKS WITH MIDFIELD.

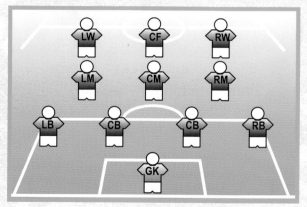

## 4–3–3
WITH ONLY 3 MIDFIELDERS THE OPPOSITION CAN ATTACK DOWN THE WINGS. SO EITHER THE FULL-BACKS HAVE TO PUSH UP OR THE STRIKERS HAVE TO DROP BACK TO HELP.

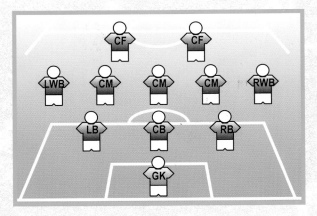

## 3-5-2

THE TWO WIDE MIDFIELDERS (WING-BACKS) HAVE TO BE VERY FIT: THEY MUST TRACK BACK TO DEFEND AS WELL AS PUSH FORWARDS TO ATTACK. THEY END UP DOING A LOT OF RUNNING!

## 3-4-3

LIKE 3-5-2 BUT WITH THE WING-BACKS PLAYING MORE DEFENSIVELY. THE TWO WING-FORWARDS CROSS THE BALL, OR COME IN TO SUPPORT THE CENTRAL STRIKER.

Colin trying to explain formations to us.

Before matches Colin tells us how he wants us to play. Things don't always go according to plan!

# SUSIE

I met an American girl called Susie in the summer at a neighbour's party. It was a good job she was there, all the others were either little kids or wrinklies.

Inbox | Compose | Addresses | Folders | Options | Print | Help

Reply | Reply All | Forward | Delete | Previous | Next | Close

From:        Susie
Date:        Friday, October 10
To:          Joe
Subject:     Soccer

>Hi Joe, Susie here!

That birthday party was pretty boring, huh? But at least I met somebody else who loves soccer.

There isn't much soccer on television over here, although we know all about David Beckham – he's cute!

Have you heard of Landon Donovan? He's like an American version of Beckham, only younger. You've probably heard of Mia Hamm. She's probably the best female player in the world. The US have a really good women's team and all us girls play it at school. It's actually the fastest growing team sport for girls here in the US. These days, even the men are pretty good. They managed to get to the quarter-finals of the last World Cup – the same as England I think.

Anyway, keep me up to date with all the football gossip over there. Hope I can come and visit next summer. Maybe I'll even get a run-out with the Dynamos!

I'll write you soon – Susie

P.S. Hope you like the pictures

>These were taken of me where we go for kickabouts, a few blocks from home. I play mostly at school, but living in Manhattan means I can sometimes go and play in Central Park. Cool, huh?

**LANDON DONOVAN**

Born: 4 March 1982

Position: Striker

Clubs: Bayer Leverkusen (Germany), San Jose Earthquakes (USA)

Donovan also played for the USA in the 2002 World Cup finals and scored two goals.

## JANUARY

| | | | |
|---|---|---|---|
| 5 | 12 | 19 | 26 |
| 6 | 13 | 20 | 27 |
| 7 | 14 | 21 | 28 |
| 1 | 8 | 15 | 22 | 29 |
| 2 | 9 | 16 | 23 | 30 |
| 3 | 10 | 17 | 24 | 31 |
| 4 | 11 | 18 | 25 | |

The Dynamos!

# SATURDAY 17 JANUARY
## MID-SEASON REVIEW

It's halfway through the season. Things are going well. I've scored eight goals in seven games! Colin (our coach) told me to shoot whenever I can, so I do — although sometimes I shoot when I shouldn't!

The Dynamos are third in the league. That's better than last year but we still let in too many goals. We need to keep more players in defence. John is still attacking too much! I suppose I could get back and help a bit more.

We don't feel so good when we lose! This was when we lost 3—2 against Rovers. They finished well below us last season but they've got a couple of new players. I think we thought we were going to win before the game even started.

When things are going well we all feel great. But we've got to be more consistent.

THINGS TO DO FOR THE REST OF THE SEASON:

· Pass a bit more. Don't ALWAYS shoot.

· Get back and help out the defence now and again.

· At least try to use my left foot.

· Learn to head the ball properly.

## MARCH

| | | | | |
|---|---|---|---|---|
| 1 | 8 | 15 | 22 | 29 |
| 2 | 9 | 16 | 23 | 30 |
| 3 | 10 | 17 | 24 | 31 |
| 4 | 11 | 18 | 25 | |
| 5 | 12 | 19 | 26 | |
| 6 | 13 | 20 | 27 | |
| 7 | 14 | 21 | 28 | |

# SATURDAY 13 MARCH TRAINING WEEKEND, DAY 1

I'm shattered! Today was the first day of the training weekend and it was really tiring, but brilliant. Hopefully by tomorrow I will have improved my game in all departments.

Now I just have to make sure I remember everything I've been taught. This bit of the diary can be a reminder for the rest of the season. I'm glad my dad came along and took photos, even though it was a bit embarrassing to have him hanging around all the time!

Training today was all about making sure our basic skills were right, so we spent the whole time practising tackling, heading the ball and kicking it accurately.

We've really learned a lot by thinking hard about the basic techniques.

Tackling.

High kick using the top of the boot.

18

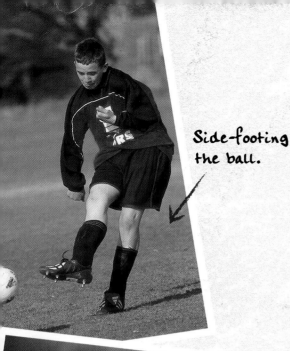

Side-footing the ball.

## TACKLING

- Try to get your body behind the ball, rather than just dangling a leg out.
- Keep your eyes on the ball.
- Commit fully to the tackle.

## HEADING TO SCORE

- Keep your eyes on the ball.
- Try to connect to the ball with your forehead (top of the head really hurts!).
- Use your arms for leverage.
- Try and attack the ball from a run up to enable you to jump higher.
- Position head slightly downwards.

## KICKING THE BALL (not the opposition!)

- Plant your standing foot (non-kicking) to help you balance.
- For accuracy, use your instep to side-foot the ball.
- For power, use the top of your boot (the laces) and kick through the ball.
- For shots or short passes, keep your head over the ball to keep it down.
- For crosses, long passes and clearances, kick underneath the ball to gain extra height.

Heading the ball.

## MARCH

| | | | | |
|---|---|---|---|---|
| 1 | 8 | 15 | 22 | 29 |
| 2 | 9 | 16 | 23 | 30 |
| 3 | 10 | 17 | 24 | 31 |
| 4 | 11 | 18 | 25 | |
| 5 | 12 | 19 | 26 | |
| 6 | 13 | 20 | 27 | |
| 7 | (14) | 21 | 28 | |

## SUNDAY 14 MARCH
## TRAINING WEEKEND, DAY 2

This second day was all about learning some more advanced skills. Everyone thinks they can dribble the ball, me included! All the tips the coaches gave us were really useful, and I'm definitely better at dribbling now than I was two days ago.

The coaches told us that some players are naturally good dribblers. Thankfully I'm one of them!

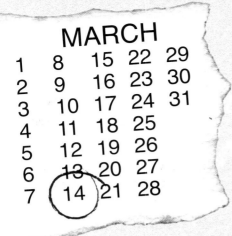

20

Attempts at overhead kicks. Not bad!

# DRIBBLING

• Keep as low to the ground as possible to stay better balanced. This should enable you to change direction or turn sharply.

• Keep the ball close to your feet (but not too close or it'll get caught under them).

• Look up so you know where your team-mates are, you might need to pass to them! A good dribbler knows when not to dribble.

# OVERHEAD (OR BICYCLE) KICK:

I've already scored with one of these, but it was a bit lucky!

• Throw your non-kicking leg in the air and follow through with your kicking leg.

• As the ball drops, try to kick it with the laces of your boot for better control.

• Keep your eyes on the ball to give you the best chance of connecting with it.

• Put your arms out to the side and slightly behind you to break your fall.

A lot of practice went on through mini-matches.

# THE WORLD CUP

I love the World Cup. I just hate having to wait for the next one to come round! The best thing is getting to watch all those great players that I don't know much about.

It would be brilliant if we won it again some day. It's amazing how excited you can get just by watching videos of past World Cups. There have been some crackers!

### 1966

The only time England have ever won the World Cup. England's stars were captain Bobby Moore and midfielder Bobby Charlton. Geoff Hurst will be always be remembered for scoring a hat-trick in the final at Wembley. England beat West Germany 4-2.

### 1974

Holland were the best team never to win the World Cup. They played 'total football' which meant defenders and attackers swapped positions regularly. Their star player and captain Johan Cruyff is one of the all-time greats. Host nation Germany beat Holland 2-1 in the final.

### 1986

Diego Maradona was the best player in the world. He led Argentina to victory, scoring five goals, including two against England in the quarter-finals. England's Gary Lineker finished top scorer with six goals.

30 July 1966 – a date every England fan knows by heart. Will we ever win the cup again?

## 1998

The host nation France won, with their star player Zinedine Zidane scoring two goals in the final against Brazil. What I remember most is Michael Owen scoring the best goal of the tournament against Argentina in the second round when he was only seventeen. Unfortunately we lost the game on penalties – again!

Michael Owen skins Almeyda of Argentina for pace. Wish I was that quick!

## 2001

Brazil made up for 1998 by winning the World Cup for the fifth time. On the way to the final, Brazil beat England 2–1 in the quarter-finals. Michael Owen scored first for England but they just couldn't hang on. Ronaldo was the Player of the Tournament with seven goals.

Amazing height from Zidane, scoring against Brazil in the World Cup final in 1998. France won 3–0.

Maradona swerves past Terry Butcher to score a great goal in the 1986 World Cup.

## World Cup Winners

1930 – Uruguay
1934 – Italy
1938 – Italy
1950 – Uruguay
1954 – West Germany
1958 – Brazil
1962 – Brazil
1966 – England
1970 – Brazil
1974 – West Germany
1978 – Argentina
1982 – Italy
1986 – Argentina
1990 – West Germany
1994 – Brazil
1998 – France
2002 – Brazil

gin Lady

## APRIL

| | | | |
|---|---|---|---|
| 5 | 12 | 19 | 26 |
| 6 | 13 | 20 | 27 |
| 7 | 14 | 21 | 28 |
| 1 | 8 | 15 | 22 | 29 |
| 2 | 9 | 16 | 23 | 30 |
| 3 | 10 | 17 | 24 | |
| 4 | 11 | 18 | (25) | |

No more
of these
for a
while!

# SUNDAY 25 APRIL
## A FOOTBALLER'S DIET

Bad news! Susie says I'm going to have to
change what I eat if I want to become a
professional footballer! I guess she knows
more about that sort of thing than I do and
if that's what it takes... Still, I don't know
how Susie expects me to go completely
without cheeseburgers! I'll give it a shot,
but I'll have to think if there are any
vegetables I like...

## SUSIE'S FOOD GUIDELINES

**WHAT'S IN**

Pasta & rice

Fish & chicken

Fruit & vegetables

Water

**WHAT'S OUT**

Hamburgers

Fries

Candy (sweets)

Fizzy drinks

Slow-burn food
provides the slow
release of energy
that is needed
for training.

From: susie
Date: Sunday, April 25
To: joe
Subject: no more hamburgers!

>Hey Joe!

Guess what? I've been doing some reading-up on what pro soccer players eat and it looks like we're both going to have to change our diets if we want to make it to the top.

We've got to eat stuff that has lots of carbohydrates and protein and is low in fat. I guess that means no more cheeseburgers and fries.

But there is some good news. You can still eat chocolate before training or a match because it contains lots of energy. It's either chocolate or bananas and I know what I'll be eating.

I've attached a list of what to eat and what not to eat. Bet you don't stick to it!

See ya
Susie

Sprinting, press-ups
and sit-ups are good for
muscle build-up.

## MAY

```
3   10  17  24  31
4   11  18  25
5   12  19  26
6   13  20  27
7   14  21  28
1   8   15  22  29
2   9   16  23  30
```

**Offside**

• When the ball is played forwards the attacker must be level with, or behind the last defender.

• A player can't be offside if the ball is played backwards.

• To be offside there must be 'daylight' between the last defender and the attacker when the ball is played.

## SUNDAY 16 MAY
## LEARNING THE RULES

I know most of the rules of football already, but there are a few I'm not 100 per cent sure about so I've been checking them out. The offside rule is important for me as I'm a striker and I get caught offside a bit too much. What matters is the attacker's position when the ball is played to him, NOT when he receives it.

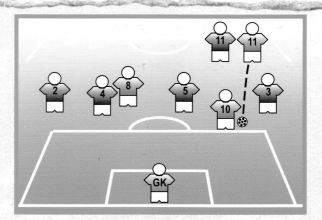

PLAYER 10 IS OFFSIDE BECAUSE HE IS IN FRONT OF ALL THE DEFENDERS EXCEPT THE GOALKEEPER.

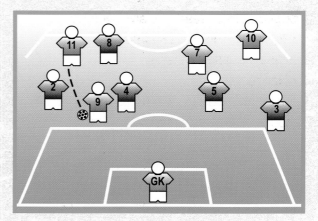

PLAYER 9 IS ONSIDE BECAUSE NUMBER 3 DEFENDER HAS NOT MOVED UP THE FIELD IN LINE WITH THE OTHER DEFENDERS.

Taking a throw-in.

I don't usually take throw-ins but it's still good to know the rules.

Preparing to take a free-kick.

## Throw-ins
• Both feet must be on or behind the line when the ball is thrown.
• Both feet must be touching the ground when the ball is thrown.
• Ball must be thrown with both hands.
• Ball must be released from behind or above the head, NOT in front.

There are direct free-kicks and indirect free-kicks. It's all a bit confusing!

## Awarding free-kicks
Free-kicks are awarded when there is foul play or misconduct.

A direct free-kick gives a team a direct shot at goal. Direct free-kicks are given for:
• Fouls (eg. kicking, tripping, pushing or jumping at an opponent).
• Handballs.
If either of these happen in the attacking team's penalty area a penalty is given.

An indirect free-kick is awarded for more minor offences. The ball has to be touched by at least two players before a goal can be scored.

DIRECT FREE-KICK

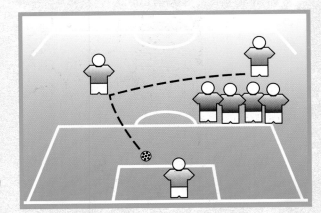

INDIRECT FREE-KICK

27

# HEROES

There are so many great players, past and present. It's hard to pick out the best but this is a pretty good selection.

## DAVID BECKHAM

(d.o.b. 2 May 1975)
**Strengths**: Passing, shooting, crossing, free-kicks, works really hard for the team
**Position**: Midfielder
**Country**: England
**Clubs**: Preston North End, Manchester United, Real Madrid
**Honours**: European Cup, Premier League, FA Cup

## RONALDO

(d.o.b. 22 September 1976)
**Strengths**: Dribbling, shooting, pace
**Position**: Striker
**Country**: Brazil
**Clubs**: PSV Eindhoven, Barcelona, Inter Milan, Real Madrid
**Honours**: World Cup, Dutch League, European Cup-Winners Cup, UEFA Cup, Spanish Cup

## PELÉ

(d.o.b. 23 October 1940)
**Strengths**: Dribbling, shooting, heading, passing
**Position**: Striker
**Country**: Brazil
**Clubs**: Santos (Brazil)
**Honours**: Two World Cups. He played in the winning team in 1958 when he was only seventeen. The 1970 team he played in was the greatest of all time.

Becks scores from the penalty spot against Turkey in 2003.

An overhead kick to end all overhead kicks! Thierry Henry beats goalkeeper Chivu of Ajax.

**MIA HAMM**

(d.o.b. 17 March 1972)
**Strengths**: Everything. The complete player
**Position**: Striker
**Country**: USA
**Clubs**: Washington Freedom
**Honours**: Has twice won the Women's World Cup with the USA

**THIERRY HENRY**

(d.o.b. 17 August 1977)
**Position**: Striker
**Strengths**: Very fast, great goalscorer (a bit like me!)
**Clubs**: Monaco, Juventus, Arsenal
**Country**: France
**Honours**: World Cup, European Championship, Premier League, FA Cup

The world's most famous female player, Mia Hamm of Washington Freedom and the USA.

# FOOTBALL LANGUAGE

## Bicycle kick
A type of volley, also known as an overhead kick. The player throws his non-kicking leg in the air and follows through with his kicking leg.

## Crossing
Passing the ball into the penalty box from the wing by the attacking team. Can be along the ground or in the air.

## Dribbling
When a player runs along with the ball at his feet and under control at all times. This usually involves taking the ball past opposition players.

## Full-back
A defender playing in a wide position as opposed to a centre-back. Can either be a left-back or a right-back.

## Hat-trick
When a player scores three goals in one game.

## Midfielder
A general term given to the players who play in between the strikers and defenders. Midfielders are expected to both attack and defend.

## Rush Goalie
When there aren't enough players to have dedicated goalkeepers, the players nearest the goal act as goalkeepers for their team, rushing back to defend the goal when necessary.

## Strikers
Players whose job is primarily to attack the opposition. Strikers are expected to score and provide goals.

## Total football
A system pioneered by Holland in the 1970s which allows players to change positions at any time. Attackers can defend and defenders can attack.

## Volley
When the ball is kicked when it is in the air, rather than on the ground.

## Wing-back
A wide player who is expected to attack and defend down one side of the pitch.